The Goldfields Thief

Story by Carmel Reilly

Illustrations by Lucy Zhang

The Goldfields Thief

Text: Carmel Reilly
Publishers: Tania Mazzeo and Eliza Webb
Series consultant: Amanda Sutera
  Hands on Heads Consulting
Editor: Holly Proctor
Project editors: Annabel Smith and
  Jarrah Moore
Designer: Jess Kelly
Project designer: Danielle Maccarone
Illustrations: Lucy Zhang
Production controller: Renee Tome

NovaStar

Text © 2024 Cengage Learning Australia Pty Limited
Illustrations © 2024 Cengage Learning Australia Pty Limited

ISBN 978 0 17 033409 9

Cengage Learning Australia
Level 5, 80 Dorcas Street
Southbank VIC 3006 Australia
Phone: 1300 790 853
Email: aust.nelsonprimary@cengage.com

For learning solutions, visit **cengage.com.au**

Printed in China by 1010 Printing International Ltd
1 2 3 4 5 6 7 28 27 26 25 24

*Nelson acknowledges the Traditional Owners and Custodians
of the lands of all First Nations Peoples. We pay respect
to Elders past and present, and extend that respect to
all First Nations Peoples today.*

Contents

Chapter 1   Thief!   5

Chapter 2   Digging and Digging   8

Chapter 3   On the Trail   12

Chapter 4   Stolen Goods   16

Chapter 5   A New Life   22

Chapter 1

Thief!

It happened – as these things often do – in a flash.

The year was 1855. Like thousands of other people, my father and I had come to the goldfields, in the colony of Victoria, to strike it rich. One day, I was on an errand in the town where we had settled when someone knocked into me.

"Watch out!" I said, turning to see a boy in a large coat running off into the crowd.

Someone behind me said, "I think that boy stole something from you."

I plunged my hand into my pocket.

"No!" I howled, on finding it empty.

I'd had Pa's pouch in my pocket. It held three small gold nuggets that we'd dug up that week. Usually, it was Pa who brought the nuggets to the gold office in town, to exchange them for money. But he was ill that day, so I'd had to go instead.

Without the money I would've got for the gold, I had no way to buy food. What was I going to do?

I reported the theft at the police station, but the constable wasn't very helpful.

"We can't do anything if we don't know who the thief is, or where he lives," he said, shrugging.

It seemed the gold was gone forever.

Chapter 2

Digging
and Digging

I trudged back to our tent, feeling terrible.
I had to tell Pa what had happened.

Pa and I had come from Wales. Since my
mother died, it was just the two of us,
and we did everything together.

On the diggings, as the goldfields were
called, we spent our days shovelling and
sifting dirt in search of gold. But so far,
we had only ever found enough to keep us
going for a few days at a time.

Pa was lying in bed with a fever. When I told him what had happened, a look of panic crossed his face.

"I'll be better soon," he muttered. "And I'll dig up some more gold. I won't let you starve, Griff."

But I knew it was me who would have to find the gold. I picked up my shovel and went outside. As I dug and dug, anger bubbled inside me. Those stolen nuggets would have bought us food for more than a week! I needed to go back to town and find the thief.

After hours of digging, I uncovered a tiny nugget. It was smaller than my smallest fingernail, but would be enough to keep us going a little bit longer.

Chapter 3

On the Trail

The next morning, Pa was still not well.
I told him I was going out to buy food.
I didn't mention that I also wanted to find
the thief.

I folded the tiny nugget I'd dug up into a
piece of cloth. This time, I tucked it into
a pocket under my coat, safe from thieves.
Then I made my way to the centre of town.

I planned to wait outside the grocery store to see if I could spot the thief in the crowd.

As luck would have it, I saw him almost as soon as I reached the store. I knew him straightaway by his large coat.

The thief went into the grocery store, and I followed.

He was only a boy, not much older than me. I had just stepped inside when I saw him take a packet of sugar from the counter while the shopkeeper was serving someone else. No one noticed as he pushed it under his coat.

The boy quickly headed out the door.
I went out after him. I'd tell the shopkeeper
about the sugar later.

The boy was easy to trail. He didn't hurry.
He must have thought he'd got away with
stealing the sugar.

I kept my distance. Soon, he left the centre
of town. After a few minutes' walk, he
entered an old, ragged tent.

Chapter 4

Stolen Goods

I was about to go and report what I had seen to the constable. But before I could move, the boy came out of the tent clutching a brown sack.

There was no time to get to the police station. I had to know where the thief was going – and what he had in that sack!

I followed him past diggers, tents and piles of dirt until I lost sight of him.
I nearly gave up, but then I spotted him heading up the small hill at the edge of town. I ran to catch up, but by the time I reached the top of the hill, he was gone.

Just as I was about to go back to town, something stopped me. Looking around, I noticed how peaceful it was up here on the hill. I didn't want to leave.

I saw that the ground was untouched by miners' shovels. *Could there be gold up here?* I wondered.

Just then, I heard a scraping noise.
I silently crept towards the sound.
Through the trees I saw the boy! He was
pushing the sack under an old log.

After a minute, he stood up and turned
in my direction. I pressed myself back
against a tree, hoping he hadn't seen me.

I held my breath.

Seconds later, I heard the boy walk off.
I went over to the log and pulled out
the sack.

Inside were pouches and purses full of gold
and coins. In among them, I saw Pa's pouch!

I hoisted the sack over my shoulder. Then
I headed to the police station.

The constable was amazed when he saw the sack with the stolen goods. As I'd already described Pa's pouch to him, and told him how much gold was inside, he let me take it straight back.

Then, he and two other constables followed me to the thief's tent.

Chapter 5

A New Life

At the tent, the constables discovered the boy, his older brother — and even *more* stolen goods!

The police took the thieves away to the police station. I didn't know what their punishment was going to be, but I was pretty sure that they wouldn't steal again.

I took my nuggets to the gold office to exchange them for money. Then I bought food.

When I returned to our tent, Pa was finally up, although he was still weak. I told him what had happened, and he hugged me tight.

"You saved the day, Griff!" he declared, a proud look in his eyes.

The *Goldfields Daily* newspaper came to interview me for a story the next morning. I was suddenly a hero for finding not only my own gold, but other people's goods as well! Some people even gave me a reward for returning their things.

When Pa was well again, I took him up to the place on the hill. He liked it, too, and we decided to move our tent there.

It turned out my feelings about finding gold were right. We soon dug up several large nuggets. We exchanged them for enough money to buy a farm and start a new life.

And, in a way, it was all thanks to the goldfields thief!